LOve Able
a poetic journey about how to love

—JULIE A. LYLE—

Seven Seas Publishing

Copyright 2023 by Seven Seas Publishing - Dr. Julie A. Lyle

All rights reserved. This book or any portion thereof may not be reproduced or used in any manner whatsoever without the express written permission of the publisher except for the use of brief quotations in a book review.

Seven Seas Publishing - Dr. Julie A. Lyle

3088 Pio Pico Drive, Suite 202, Carlsbad, CA 92008

www.drjuls.com

Print ISBN: 979-8-9894551-0-2

Love yourself. Then forget it.

Then, love the world.

MARY OLIVER

INTRODUCTION

Nine journals are stacked. Thick voluminous parchment layers, I open the first, then second, to the ninth. Innings of my life, I sense a devotion, a reverence, to the decades tumbling out across thousands of scribbles.

From age 15 to 55, I narrated the losses, gains and strains on my heart with words bound together. Even though eyesight is not as keen after forty, wisdom arrives in the capacity to see the bigger picture. Poised at a table, sequestered with a laptop in a rickety mountain cottage, recurrent cups of PG Tips, ten of my favorite CD's, a few beers and overdue determination, I open and reread each and every one.

Page after page chronicled life stories, mine and others. I revisited episodes when I was an au-pair in France and desperately missing my home and first love. Another splayed the distressful self blame of a misguided brief first marriage. The years merged from renewed trust in meeting my knight, to nauseating procrastination of my creativity, to euphoria of motherhood and the agony of my dad's death. Some captured the angst of emotional black holes, life events spoke to me in trembling ways, demanding I capture the experience as a photographer does with a click.

A profound meaning took shape. Every entry, unbeknownst to my twenty, thirty or even forty something self, was documenting how I acquired the power, skill and ability to love, face inadequacies, absorb joy, overcome fears and keep on moving on. How are we able to love? How does loving become possible? Perhaps being "love able" has less to do with how we act, look or think and more about becoming competent in our ability to be vulnerable, generous, brave, persistent and honest.

And so I ask myself, why now? Why undress and reveal these inner reflections, why get naked in this display of intimate documentation? Perhaps I don't want to hide the words any longer. Seclusion closely approximates shame, and I have no time for the burden of embarrassment. Confidence is born from reducing the power of others to diminish, hurt or take away joy. And so, gratitude trickles steadily as you, the curious reader, deposit precious time to visit these pages. I am sincerely appreciative, humbled and hopeful you will discover a few of your own love abilities resonating within.

— Juls

StAGES of Contents

YouthFULL

It Is	7
Souvenirs	8
Channeling Joni	10
Shifting	11
Fast Forward	12
Mind, Body, Soul and Heartbreak	13

Faux Grown Up

Liberty	17
InCOMPASSing	18
The Man Plan	19
Chaos	20
Bad Grief	22
Physical Therapy	23
Lily	24
A Wakening	26

Taking the Leap to Deep

Passion 29
Contra-Diction 30
Ups and Downs on Writers BLOCK 31
Co-Dependent Flood 32
Leprechaun Love 33
The Gifts 34
BB - Before Baby 35
Six Weeks 36
Christmas Morn Again 38
Battleground Snooze 39
Got Milk 40

Heart Hiccups

Come Out and Play! 43
Shall We Dance? 44
The Unlikely Hood 45
Miss Diagnosis 46
The Knowing Game 47
Renewing the Vows 48
Me Time 49
Les Soeurs 50

Facing Nature

Bienvenue Hiver	53
The Bamboo Heart	54
New Years ReSOULutions	55
Come, Gather Your Soul	56
Saving Daylight	57
Death Mask	58
North Shore	59
Sucia	60
Denouement	61

Aging Grace

Forty-Three Days	65
On the Edge of 40	66
Circle of Love	67
Lost Little Girl	69
Rescue Mission	70
The Last of the Firsts	71
So	72
Becoming 50	73
Soul Aboard	75
The Beat Goes On	76
Evening Song	77
Mid-Morning Tea	78
The Bridge	79
Bodaica	81

YouthFULL

Ahhh, how sweet it was and wasn't

It is…

Mesmerized by your glance
Fascination sweeps through
At every touch, word, clue
It is you.

Excitation overruled the past
advancing toward tomorrow
omnipresent sorrow
It is me.

Clouding cyclic style
Floating into one another's joys
Unmeasurable is life's ploy
It is us.

Bringing it down so easy
Ceasing only the farthest star's light
Propelling admiration to its height
It is love.

August, 1977

Souvenirs

I know I can let it out now
No regrets, I smile
Satisfied to be here
Having conquered a weathered fear
Alone, but far from lonely

Summer had not taken flight
I packed my bags, said goodbye
Unknowing of what lay ahead
Missing someone to share my bed

What a long time it seemed from
Dinner through caffeine
London took me from the sky
First impressions don't lie

Memories of England
People, places, palaces, parks and style
The food appealed to me
Concerns were set free
A week only, calls me back all the while

Leaving out of Victoria Station
Bags more than needed
A boy named Vince, carried me away
From train, to boat, to the port at Calais
Together, fate can be kind.

I remember looking from the window
Train moving past fields, different air
On French ground
Starting to lose what I'd found
Back on the quay, back in time

Funny how God sends His sign
The sky, it cried
The rain came down
As I reached Paris town
I gave a smile but cried like the clouds.

JUNE, 1978

Channeling Joni

Farewell to Paris, au revoir to June
Leaving, oh leaving, didn't come too soon
Hello to another place, hello to tears
Why do these minutes pass away like years?
I'm waiting, waiting to come home to you
Keeping my head up, there's nothing else to do
Denied you the love to share long before
California, oh California, I'm knocking at your door.

July, 1978

Shifting

Trapped, flat, pushed back
Against a wall of love
Bound by your possessions
Strapped with an iron glove
I can't breathe, sneeze, lay down
Without a thought of you
Haunting my existence
My heart, what can I do?
You bought a ring, song, setting
So well planned
I struggle against your steady stand
You shout, spout, declare
Eternal bliss for us
A schism swarms around me
I'll be riding the same time but on a different sphere
I'm coming home, but changed.
So convenient to blame,
So I've shackled my heart.
Adventure seemed a foreign invader to us, now my old friend.
What do I have left to trust?

SEPTEMBER, 1979

Fast Forward

Don't tell me, they've taken your feathered earrings
Given you a gold necklace, a charm for your age,
loves and what you like to eat best.
Remember those days when Barbie and Ken were the only best friends?
Oh, why do you have to grow up? Why do you have to grow up just yet?

Wait a minute, where's your torn t-shirt
those shorts more holier than thou?
They've given you a suit, tie and tennis gear.
Yesterday a Big Wheel took you to any place you wanted to be.
Oh, why do you have to grow up? It's all happening too rapidly.

One push on a swing and you were flying for hours
A ball and bat was a Saturday afternoon
This growing up, it's happening too soon.

Oh GI Joe where did you go?
To that battlefield of boxes in the garage.
Those moments of stardom before the mirror,
a Raider with Paul Revere.
This growing up, do you have to do it so fast?

It happens every day,
the years they slip away.
I'll always wonder why we have to grow up at all?

AUGUST, 1980

Mind, Body, Soul and Heartbreak

Turn your head away
Your eyes can't stand the light
Heart is pounding
Stomach turns
Nothing ever right again

Come to my window for a killing
Step up to the glass and break
On the brink, your fists tight
Past sweeps through, memories hide
Clouding the view, but you know what is inside

Once happy, but what means happiness now
Piles of hurt for a young soul to bare
Not enough smiles for your face to wear
Too old for your days
Knowing you can never go back
Only the tears push reality away

Come to my window for a killing
Step up to the glass and break
Leaving the curtains of your mind aside

Watch as the whole become parts
Shattered and fallen
You can't put it back
The pieces only cut

You realize you won't replace this transparent shield
You'll try for awhile to see how the breeze feels

JANUARY, 1981

14

Faux Grown Up

*A very misplaced "I do"
and way too many "I wills"*

Liberty

Wishing for things changed but gone
Leave me hanging
Threads breaking the winds of time
Granting freedom to the prisoner, my heart
And yet I continue to harbor the fugitive, my dreams

Broken, in need of repair.
Searching for starlight at dawn
Hanging on to the hope within a fantasy of tomorrow
Today was never here, but gone.

September, 1985

InCOMPASSing

Look to the west and wonder what is best
Look to the east for the most or the least

Follow the wind, the sun will set again
Who will borrow tomorrow?

Passing days,
adjustments to lasting ways
my heart has joined yours
Strange how everything you say
has the answer within or without
Will you borrow tomorrow?

You look right
I scream my fright
I look left
you plead, you guess
Will I borrow tomorrow?

If I follow where you go
the dawn will only show
if I borrow tomorrow

JUNE, 1990

The Man Plan

I had a strategy
a plan to win
I had everything to hope for
great dreams
I was the director
you the actor, script in hand
you seemed ready
to take every command

If only you had stayed to the script
If only time had not been the belligerent edit
If only I had not held on so fiercely
for you to complete the scene
If only's only remind me
of what we could have been

Now everywhere I look
I see smiles but not mine
Driving, walking, I see others' happy gains
I see people making the best
and so, I have a screen up called pain.

Couples–I see couples in step.
Dancing together, compatible, in sync.
Hopeful and accepting
I see through my pain
and other people's gains.

What I have lost. I'm lost. We are lost.

APRIL, 1992

CHAOS

When you left, fate began.
Life reflected chaos.

Clothes stacked and thrown.
Towels, damp and useless.
Dishes slammed against leftover residue.
Phone calls unanswered.

Papers, bills, letters, newspapers;
life stuck unopened in despair.

Slowly, I prodded, reached deep
to find order, purpose, energy, discovery, meaning and
momentum. I began to sense the need to touch,
feel and belong to our space which lost
me in its chaos, its pain, its quicksand of bitterness.

Each day, a robotic decision to walk, talk and get
through. Day 5, making my bed, smoothing the crumbling
sheets without you. Cleaned out my jewelry box and cupboards.
Found the top of my desk, I began to catch a glimmer of me.

Not a lot of tears this first week. Long and quick
glimpses in my heart of sadness, such sadness of what
I wished could have come true.
A Wizard of Oz analogy, I've woken up to find no place
to call home outside of myself, I am so scared.
Alone, yet free of debt from a staggering emotional loan.

Free to work, to play, to create without editing
through his loss or fear, where has love gone?
Am I asleep in my needs and expectations?
Am I going to wake up and find that I've thrown the home away?
How to be true to me?

It begins by picking up clothes, sorting laundry,
staring at the ceiling and myself
dusting off one shelf at a time.

SEPTEMBER, 1992

Bad Grief

Through the eyes of grief...
The entire planet seems to be having a
great time, a party, and I wasn't invited.

Through the eyes of grief...
Everyone has found love,
there is none left for me.

Through the eyes of grief...
Everyone seems to have a big laugh over a wonderful joke,
and I don't get the punchline.

Through the eyes of grief...
How dare the world continue on when it hurts just to open
my eyes and face another day without me.

OCTOBER, 1992

Physical Therapy

Meeting men is like working out,
you either feel refreshed, energized or exhausted.
Torn ligaments and sweat pouring down each encounter.

I sprained my intelligence tonight.
Stumbled over my uncomfortableness,
I fled from the rubble.

I made myself awkward with my truth
I have landed on another planet and don't know how to breathe.

Am I just waking up to the truth I have been a coward for so long?
Running away from men and life,
I spent the weekend in Los Angeles. Eye contact is getting easier.

What do I have to learn about me? Everything.

DECEMBER, 1992

Lily

I picked a flower from a book,
named it mine forever.
I watered it with hopes and plans
dreams of what it would deliver.
Believed it was the one
imperfect but withstanding,
the tests of time made real
optimism my landing.

I filled myself with wasted fear,
shed the cloak of judgment.
I watered and adhered
to every need the plant indulgent.
Saw myself the great jardiniere
with every tool at hand,
but the one I could not give the plant
was the desire, on his own, to stand.

I dreamed the flower from my heart
held onto what could be.
So fiercely I began to lose sight,
my sacrifice meant neglecting me
You see, I watered with my time,
ideas and skill.
I watered with laughter and with glee.
I watered until my cup ran dry
and had none left to give to me.

I lived my life
believing I was to water other's seeds,
so they would grow strong, beautiful and proud;
a work of art for others to take heed.
Now I know there is no other flower,
no tools to make someone feel their worth.
I cannot assume the job
to take care of someone else's birth.

Aha, I look and found my seed inside,
a flower to bloom.
I alone must water my soul out of doom.
I look now and see
a lovely rose, a blossoming flower, staring back at me,
I am free to grow.

December, 1992

A Wakening

It rolls in, a velvet dew curtain during
early morning stirrings,
eclipsing the night, a stealth invader.
It alters the climate of familiarity;
a chill to be denied, dismissed.
It stirs, an irritating nudge to complacency.

"Wake up" it whispers.
Fear makes heavy the eyelids.
Pull the covers up, hit the snooze button,
lay still, play dead and make its recurrence illicit, unwanted.

Silence instinct and there will be no bumping into walls,
or tumbling into pits.
Only inevitable wrinkles of blame and what if's.

We paper mache with history and habits;
 lumpy layers of loyalty to others, flammable glue.
"Damaged" becomes the label, emotionally inked.

"Wake up" the tone demanding.
Yanking off the covers, painfully exposed,
the place from which disappointment breeds.
"WAKE UP" the relentless messenger,
the soul's drill sergeant losing patience!
To linger is to submit to terminal regret.
To sit up, swing legs over the edge,
reach into the thick unknown...tapping toes forward,
seeking a surface to trust, to grope, breathe, and
proceed into the abyss of change...this is to be alive.

JANUARY, 1993

Taking the Leap to Deep

La Mere dans moi

PASSION

Passion explodes and we find ourselves in each other
Words attach to waves of emotion and I am captured

But what do I, how much do I, reveal to this new man who is sharing so much with me?

Honesty is a strange bedfellow and I cautiously touch its presence.

FEBRUARY, 1993

Contra-Diction

I run a bath each night, wishing to float away.
I watch you naked wishing you'd look my way.
I tell jokes and struggle with my own ego.
I have all the answers, only for others.
I want to do something unpredictable, I want to stay home.
I say "Bitch", I read the Bible.
I drink champagne, I take vitamins.
I walk loudly, I meditate.
I paint walls and collect angels. I question my faith.
I accept my friends, I find all my faults.
I talk fast, I have been stuck for years.
I am funny, I cry myself to sleep.
I want to run away, I have $57.82 in my bank account.
I am a truth seeker, I go through red lights.
I love feathers, I am heavy.
I adore children, I don't have my own.
I am a woman of substance fighting emptiness.
I am a bucket of contradictions pouring out.

FEBRUARY, 1996

Ups and Downs on Writers BLOCK

so many words laboring to be born
so little time to just be
so much torment
while the ocean sleeps
where am I to go when I weep?

nowhere to smile
so much that waits to be released
to dispel this pain
leaves me empty and without
where am I to go when I shout?

desperate searching in this cerebral pantry
clever, never before used ingredients
then clutching within seconds what is expired
sensing the arrival of a distant whine
repeat performances have no audience
lost in an emotional forest of the sublime

have I foresaken what is mine?
I am a pendulum with a tired battery

OCTOBER, 1996

Co-Dependent Flood

Quick, get the toolbox from underneath the sink,
I'm in need of fixing the way I act, feel and think!
My energy is leaking into everyone else's gaps
If I don't reclaim me, I'll bend, strain, I'll snap

So hand me the screwdriver,
I've got bolts to undo
I'm freeing loose ends
to my own heart be true

AUGUST, 1998

Leprechaun Love

The past.
Stepping stones
leading to our hearts

The seeds.
Watering time
allowing us to grow

True commitment.
The glue
holding our dreams

Your love.
Carries me
beyond the rainbow

Lucky me.
My pot of gold.

FEBRUARY, 1999

The Gifts

We have had trials,
moments when we are broken and torn.
We cry tears when pain reigns.
In these times we sigh
knowing all is not lost.
For friends are the gifts that we gain.

Some carry the load,
when life hands you burdens.
Others are the reflection, when memory fades.
Some give you wings,
when your legs tire.
Friends are reminders of the life we have made.

Others are your voice, if silence befalls you.
Lighting candles of hope,
if future vision becomes slight.
They are the heart,
when strife leaves you longing,
the gifts so blessed, so right.

APRIL 24, 1999

BB-Before Baby

Thoughts on baby…
Days, hours, minutes.
Time pours out with the
consistency of pea soup.
Slow, waiting to
digest this new reality.
This new me and you.

MARCH 3 (*8 days before birth*), 2000

Six Weeks

the wonder of it all I am left wordless
the abundance of emotion staggering
and the description lacking form
how to capture the metamorphosis of me
through loving you?

amazing face
your eyes dart to another dimension
and I am humbled by all I will never know
that somehow you possess an understanding.
simple needs and I am hungry to fill them all
a new desperation to defy harm and ugliness
to will away future pain.
how in the world could I have ever believed
that I was complete outside of you?

I hold you against my chest
my heart which sustained you
now we are partners
as if I have known you forever, in my soul.
was every step I stumbled and every moment
I conquered just pushing me to this inevitable purpose?
was there a plan, a quota of trusting to reach?
I sit for hours, days and now six weeks,
suspended between the mystery and truth of you.
Your beauty is unending and there is no greater comfort
than dancing to your smile as it sings to me.
that you are exactly where you belong
and so am I.

how odd to not intuit I was waiting for this gift!
that while longing silently, subconsciously,
what if fear had prevented me from this venture?
resulting in perhaps a staggering punishment to be reflected
for knowing what I know now, the most damning life sentence
would have been to deny myself this joy.

I am abundantly grateful to be
so completely, totally, monumentally
in love with you,
my son, my darling boy, Thomas.

APRIL 27, 2000

Christmas Morn Again

Blue eyes
capturing movement
discovery within each moment.
What do you see?
Forests in the wood blinds?
Bears dancing in the wind?
Angels in the clouds?
Your eyes penetrate empty spaces,
what do you find there?
My heart soars
your blue eyes land on me.

Do you see how I adore you?
It is Christmas morn again and again.
A gift unwrapped and treasured…
every time your blue eyes find me.

A smile blooms
and you are watered by my joy.
Just when I thought I could love no more,
I am pulled farther, deeper and harder into you.

I will never be lost to you,
I will be as constant as the sky.
How could I have ever imagined
the rightness of having you?

I hold each moment precious,
your hands grow and grip my soul.
I will always love you like no other.
I am so blessed to be your mother.

MAY, 2000

Battleground Snooze

Fighting sleep, the diapered warrior
with a vengeance you refuse to weaken.
Turning, twisting, curiosity your weapon
desire your shield, you strive to stay awake.
Pulling, tugging at my face, exploring my
nostrils as caverns.
I lay there still, a quiet frontier to discover each night.
Patience brings victory,
your breathing steadies, your probing softens,
the warrior is fading as the angel falls asleep.

November 27, 2000

Got Milk?

drying up...
where did the milk go?
the apparatus is sitting idly
without purpose
the nightly ritual of "pumping"
fading away
these stages of development and departure,
leave me feeling a longing that takes me off guard
each step of growth decreases dependency on me,
yet increases my need for him to need me.

My body is responding to his adaptation
as he eats and feasts more on the world around him,
I am not the sole provider.
A woman who counts herself as
intelligent and insightful,
I am as fragile as a leaf floating on the stream
and the rapids are coming.

I must brace for each new wave of uniqueness,
the bond during these past eight months is beyond literary expression.
the comfort, calm and familiarity that became second nature
as I held, fed and wrapped my baby in me.
and now, I am drying up, challenged to feed him in other ways,
trust that my love will hold him to me as he feeds on life's possibilities,
hope that he will always know that as he grew from me first at delivery
and now from the breast, our hearts will forever be intertwined.

JANUARY, 2001

Heart Hiccups

As close as close can be

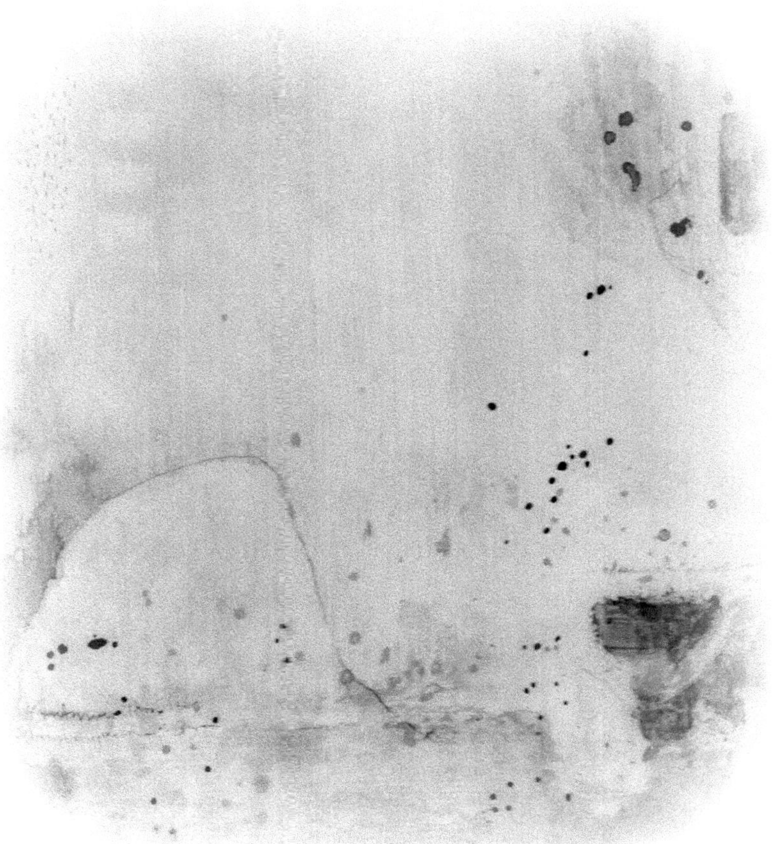

Come out and play!

come, see
the clouds have lifted
blue parchment shapes
I am waking up to find me

come, play
bounce in the pillows of surrender
swing high, courage pushes you
beaming tears of joy

come, listen
sway to the whistle of truth
hum a tune of possibilities
dance to the rhythm of wonder

come, rejoice
march in your own parade
forging a path in the field
shouting…I am! I am!

January, 1999

Shall We Dance?

One, two, three, left right left.
Dance with me, spin the tale
Familiar safety patterns,
complicated strategy
stepping on toes.

The music begins,
loud and lust-full.
We embrace the hope,
humming our own tunes.
Bumping shoulders with partners from the past,
the floor becomes crowded with hurts, memories, needs.

One holds tightly,
the other pulls back.
Movement paralyzed,
the melody strained, distant.

Does the dance grow exhausting?
Can we find synchronicity?
Do we crumble in a puddle of anger on the floor of love?
Or do we learn to tango differently?

July, 1999

The Unlikely Hood

Going inward, losing momentum
waves of questions and turmoil
where to find me?
Close to tears - courting fears
to come out from this unlikeli-hood

So what to say
when all else fails
to follow through, pass the doubt
only time is left standing

The night holds a quiet cloud
The phone doesn't wake
Desperate to escape this noisy anguish
the soul quakes

Going inward and losing ground
I stumble to the point of no return
I must find me
Beyond the cheers - raging years
beneath this unlikeli-hood

FEBRUARY, 1999

Miss Diagnosis

Where can she be, where did she go?
When will she get here if she lives in the past?
Oh Miss Diagnosis, the shattered ego, the struggling id.
A tear for you, a tear for me, but who will cry last?

What can we call her that she will come?
Self-discovery infers you don't want to be lost.
But Miss Diagnosis, with her ups and downs
finds comfort in burden, no matter the cost.

The agony of defeat brings calm to the storm
change is the jealous lover, time.
Face the music, where is the melody of repair?
Yet, there is no voice within, abuse makes the mime.

Searching through choices as a pirate looks for gold.
Taking prisoners, perpetuating grief.
Ah, Miss Diagnosis, labeling the pain without the remedy.
When will the captive heart be released?

MAY, 2001

The Knowing Game

chilling to pause long enough
descend to the basement of instinct
webs of memory, gossamer dread
force the reunion of avoidance versus truth

hidden, shrouded behind smiles and busy piles
mounds of doing to be bent, kicked and netted
score one for her.

straining, lean into the treasure chest, hoist the lid
splintered not destroyed, damn the clutter of all unsaid
every knowing packed away, diminished, fleeting
amid the plight of being right,
still a pulse to be touched, revived and heard
score two for her.

tumbling to the sanctuary, scars, emotional tattoos
honored not shamed, beauty is in the eyes of the essential woman
carrying herself to safety, transformed, authentic timely rescue
collects her heart and starts, breathing out and in
to be the knowing one
Win.

OCTOBER, 2002

Renewing the Vows

What would it be like to be new again in your eyes?
To be impatient with desire.
To not be able to sleep, or keep,
Every song from being sung for you.

What would it take to be a beautiful mystery?
Wanted, held with pure perfection
the object that awakens your passion.

What would it take to shake this polite sheet that covers us?
Disguised as comfort, familiar controlled calm.
It weighs heavy, soiled with what we used to be.
Have all the colors faded?

What would it mean to go
beyond where we've arrived –
Having disembarked at the wrong station, deserted, lost.
Are we stranded, unable to find one another?

Phases, you say, stages are natural.
Yet, practice makes perfect and
you have no curiosity left for me.

Glimpses of breathless, long kisses linger from another life.
Resignation has punctured hope, deflated my heart.
How long this shared intimate paralysis?
'Til death do us part?

FEBRUARY, 2006

Me Time

I keep leaving my inner life and then it calls me back,
a voice, angry, irritated and longing to be calmed.
"Why do you constantly, with such predictability, leave me to rot?"
It is a fierce, demanding voice of my creativity.
It is the scream of my hopes. How, why, do you desert me?

I fear I will leave my mark on this world with the insignia,
"I ran out of time."
It brings a slight, soft smirk to my face. How dramatic.
How pathetic to victimize myself with the calendar.

April, 2009

Les Soeurs

Walls dressed with smiling faces
So close and yet so far
Where mysteries line scrapbooks
the doors of time left ajar.

Is there magic in the journey?
Bridges are fragile when made of clay
the sculptor's cruel joke, nature's vision
Misunderstanding washes them away.

There is a fine line when love is the pen
And the script is tangled and torn
The remnants of battles and twisted regrets
Wounds from where two sides of one soul were born.

June, 2009

Facing Nature

How delicately sweet and mysteriously sturdy it is

Bienvenue Hiver

Winter was served up cold today,
on a platter of rain and wind.
With a scratchy itch in the throat,
that spicy cider hums better.

The season is moving faster,
with each passing spray of starlight and thunder.
Bits of Christmas music dance across air waves
and strangers don't seem so strange,
for winter brings the warmth out in humanity.

With the winds, the rain, the heater turned on.
I know I am leaving behind the fall of my marriage,
and the denouement of my life's script.

I welcome the breath of cool hope
that my world is blowing me
towards such bright Springs.

And I ride the winter night out
listening to the voice of my soul, on this,
a December eve.

Beckoning that I settle myself in
for it will only be as long a winter as the storm may need.

December, 1992

The Bamboo Heart

Open and ready
no longer holding onto fear
it brings no safety

Bending with each
new breeze of change
life's force fills me

Confident, graceful
I stand tall and sure
my inner peace
a posture for security

Humble, available to
hear and feel the
lessons of life

Swaying a beautiful
dance of hope
this is my discovery
this is my purpose

Healing wounds
singing praises to opportunities
creating my best self
accepting truth

The power to know
who you are and rejoice
Where the path starts
is through the Bamboo Heart

APRIL, 1997

New Years ReSOULutions

Watching the waves of emotion hit sands of despair
The last two weeks have brought clarity
I keep myself in prison,
the relentless warden
Refusing parole
I have told myself there is nowhere but the cage to go.

And now, the keys revealed, the storm passing
I will release me, my sentence served
To my own heart be true

What a wondrous gift to hold dreams in ones palm
Fear has shrouded the treasure
I possessed all along

Knowledge is power, but self knowledge is love
as each wave finds the shore
voices of courage say "Open the door!"

A new year answers questions that became a self defeating chant-
no more room for hopelessness, no more "I can't."

Only beauty in a gateway unlocked
a sunset, the first horizon
Where my heart, body, soul and mind
find safe harbor and dock.

January 1, 1998

Come, Gather Your Soul

August packed its days
Stowing them in September
The sun hides early
Morning skies vivid with a calling
Sharpens breezes
Subtle chills
A new wardrobe discovered in the trees
Crescent moon
Summer farewells
Resolutions registered
Flowers blessed us
Scrapbooks await
Beaches abandoned
Seasons slide along
Swift, yet ours to command
Welcome autumn, young yet wise
Gather inspiration
Carry us to the next page
To read life's mystery of our
Harvest.

SEPTEMBER, 2000

Saving Daylight

*Fresh, smooth breezes
Welcome Spring*

*Shed the bustle of resolutions
and the negligence of daylight
as now we greet the blooms.*

*What was planted on the twelfth night
a seedling of imagination
a whisper of what could be
beckons us to embrace beginnings.*

*When first we glimpse
shadows caress and host
pedals of possibilities
rainbows of wonder*

*All hail the plush greens,
summer has yet to dry
Inhale cool, pinched air
winter's lingering good-bye.*

APRIL, 2003

Death Mask

Rain pelted, striking down
smothering the ground in tears.
Nature emitting its empathy or wrath,
for the suffering or faults of its visitors.

Fall blistered, hardened,
scarring smooth sands of time.
Mortality arriving with a warning,
no mystery, only denial.

Holidays cascaded, belittling joy,
demanding cheer battled avoidance.
Happiness the only image, smiles
to keep others protected.

January settled, a parachute of days
urging toward acceptance.
Farewell sounding a hallow echo
in the empty well of my heart.

JANUARY, 2005

North Shore

Perfect calm, perfection…catalog and remember this.
Flip flops half buried, driftwood scattered
like broken glass on tile.
Breezes brush the back of my neck, a slightly cool
massage or whisper.
Sea chants with every whish against the shore
Meaty crabs fleeing dry land
Magnificent orange beachball bouncing on the horizon,
dodging the clouds as it leaves our day to begin
someone else's.
The portrait left of oranges, blues, hues of unclaimed names
Changing sketches, oh the beauty and marvel of this,
the ending of a perfect day.

August, 2012

Sucia

A floor of water
Sea bath stretching as far east as west
Sounds, sways. silences abound
tranquility exacted

With perfection in each stem
Pristine mineral sculptures
Rising out, mounds of history
Fossilized ridged tales

Shadows answer gravity
Tides paint the salty canvas
Spontaneous grids dance and flee
Escaping the watchful eye

Not a floor, a ceiling
Thriving enchantment
I am but a minuet observer
Of this vast marvelous mystery

June 11, 2016 (*Eastsound*)

Denouement

Timeless clouds linger, cushions the sky, its bed.
Still as deer perched and watchful,
above a Mohave of liquid glass
forever as it was, is now.

Majestic silhouettes, stoic arms outstretched,
praising the day's denouement.
Assembled as a faithful tribe,
forever as it was, is now.

Final whistles, tender calls,
winged reminders beckon safe home.
The sun heeds and departs,
forever as it was, is now.

June 11, 2016 (*Eastsound*)

AGING GRACE

*Age is an idea, a reality, an illusion,
a destiny, our legacy*

Forty-Three Days

Just the other day, or was it years ago?
You glimpsed a vision in the clouds,
a Goddess may have not been far
from where one day, you'd see
unexpected miracles often are wrapped in life's mystery.

Your life is a wondrous collection
of moments that you own.
Today marks twenty-four thousand and ninety days (24,090) that
your star has shown.
If each day is a reminder of the love we have to hold,
then each day is a birth-day and we cannot grow old.

Forty-three days ago, you were forced
to add something new,
to the fine heart collection that encapsulates you.
These forty-three days are mere specks on the mosaic of your life
Forty-three days of colors called pain, shock and strife.
Yet, looking closely at these unwanted shades of grief
there are surprising new hues of faith, joy and relief.

Just the other day, or just a moment ago?
You paused to look in your soul
and saw the angels living there.
Life granted; yesterday a certainty, today a possibility,
tomorrow unknown.
Fragile gifts each moment – never a birth not shown.

DECEMBER 3, 1998

On the Edge of 40....

Dig deep to find the coolness of what is underneath
Feeling the granules, crystals, gold
Reaching the reality of now.

Cradled in the open, outdoor womb
If the wind is let in
I will decide where it is to blow.

In my reality
The dawn of readiness
The stardust lilies waking up
The rainbows smell of fresh paint
I am alive.

On the edge of 40
Looking back to where I am
I cut myself up
In colorful pieces
To fill the mosaic where it was blank
Dark, painful clouds
The thunder roared within
On the edge of 40
And now, I begin.

FEBRUARY 6, 1999

Circle of Love

You dressed me up in a silly wabbit costume.
Bathed me in joy and splendor.
Pinks and plaids,
through the good and bad,
I am your daughter forever.

You held my hand, held my heart.
promised me comfort through pain.
Braids and bows,
the smiles and woes.
I am thanking you once again.

You woke me each day.
encouraged each victory.
Hopscotch to ice skates,
through the bumps and scrapes
so blessed, how you have loved me.

You gave me a map when I was lost in fear.
Your understanding a song to my silence.
Acceptance and patience,
through learning and tears,
I have found the woman in me thanks to your guidance.

So what to wrap up, and have you discover,
on this, your birthday celebration?
What to give to you for all your dedication?

I will give you wings,
when your legs may tire.
I will be your voice, if silence falls.
I will light candles,
if sight becomes shaded.
I will be here to answer your call.

I will carry the load,
when life hands you burdens.
I will be the reflection when memory fades.
I will be the heart,
when love leaves you longing.
I will give you back all the gifts that you gave.

December, 1999

Lost Little Girl

Where does it go, all this aching?
When does it end, this pinching of my heart?
I am simply a child in the face of this grief.

And it rocks slowly, as the drifting in of the sea.
Daily chores, robotic smiles and the return to what others need.
The absence of my recovery leads them to face their own fear,
their unique version of inevitable agony.

"She is really taking it hard" can only be murmured by the lonely;
I pity them, sad children inside adult masks, never protected or adored.
They are without the gift when death comes with a phone call and they
hang up and continue to play.

Just a minute while I moan, contorted in this unspeakable loss,
wringing all the innocence from my gut,
I pray I spring back forever changed.

There is no room for anger and I don't know if "yet" belongs.
Time will tell, just as it did today, one month from the Irish wake and
I am in darkness, suspended in this permanent eclipse of overlapping
sadness and overwhelming pity for my crumpled, pierced heart.

October, 2004

Rescue Mission

And with a single resonance there came a rumble,
pulse beating, gush of change.
Hurling the known into a desperate abyss;
Unsettling the fantasy of impenetrable calm
of what was so comfortably our life.

Barely standing as our hearts quake and then break
Everything on the shelves of our happiness altered.
Torture, moment to moment endurance
Our family story brings us to an anguished "Good-bye."
We crumble, descend into the obscurity of grief, not able to face the damage.

And with a single resonance there came a stirring,
"We're here for you," softly nudging us to come back.
"It is too painful, this hole is too deep," we echoed from despair.
"Take hold of our wings and we'll help you out," and we were lifted.

With constant attention to the injury,
each phone call, card, message and gift
tender bandages placed to help us heal.
Attention to absolute care, the angels worked their wonder.
And we began to walk, tentatively from our misery.

Our angels sit before us, sipping a glass of wine.
As their experience dictated most intimately, we now must allow time.
And so it is with a single resonance, "Hey, how are you doing? It's me."
There comes a glimmer, a beckoning to forge on,
blessed with angel friends, our heartaches' true remedy.

DECEMBER, 2004

the last of the firsts

how many times to bid farewell
the agony grows with the depth of forever
and the pain steeps, floating darker

desperation, unknown
no more counting of a week or a month since
the moment life diverted from innocence

and now, goodbyes are echoed in between

September, 2005

so…

so this is it,
when mortality is just a phone call away
with a ring tone piercing our denial
the ultimate fallibility of our prayers, fantasies and childlike wishes

so here it is,
the observation of sunsets, no green flash, just floods of memories
when we were so small, so far from our own horizon
and now sit, closer than before to the quickness of our days

so now it is,
the day-to-day functions, forging past the dread
and yet perhaps it becomes more of what is,
our breathing becoming more accustomed
to the shock of saying "goodbye"
the inevitability not being quite such a harsh sentence
and yes, wading farther out, the water being more comfortable
than we once believed.

APRIL, 2008

Becoming 50

What is a number?
The stroke marks competing with mortality's scoreboard?
For the first time I am aware of my place on the field,
and how I am winning.

I am deeply committed to who and what I love,
every moment of every moment.

I am aware when I am multitasking phone and e-mails and I say
"Talk to you later," I may not, so I pause to savor the humanity I
am honored to touch, hear and be connected to.

I am anxious about numbers and their endpoint inevitability, and
yet at peace with what I cannot control.

Years ago I did not believe I could endure grief or the departure of
loved ones. Now, I know, I am still not willing but able.

I diligently pop vitamins, yet I secretly know they are just
a placebo to fate.

The more I like myself, the more I become comfortable with not
trying to appeal and dance fast enough for those who don't like me.

I am the magician. I know the truth about this birthday trick.
And when those younger try to console or educate me on "it's just a
number," I smile knowingly. They have not joined this club yet.

I relish the wisdom, the joyful abandon of realizing love is not about making my husband more like me, but rather liking more of me and loving him for making me his world.

It is with absolute certainty that I know my favorite time of the day; stroking my Tommy's head as he sleeps, watching his eyelids dance as he dreams.

I no longer aim to be funny, smart, successful or beautiful enough. I now am.

FEBRUARY, 2009 (*thanks Eiji*)

Soul Aboard

Running to myself
Kidnapping my soul
Coming back to here
Staying means I must go

Packing my bags
With pieces of my heart
Seeking the reflection
Destiny from the start

Buying a one-way ticket
Traveling swift on the storm of time
So many stops for useless pain
The passport is deemed mine

Running to my truth
The captain a merciful guide
Shedding light on old harbors
Where my fears can no longer hide

I am the ship
'God's speed' says my soul
As I lift my anchor.

June, 2010

The Beat Goes On

Where do we go when the heart stops?
When one still beats and the other is beyond?
Is the heart and soul divorced or one?
The muscle it ceases, the soul remains.
Reflecting love embodied, reclaimed.

Being the force to bring forth
all that is true, real, safe, protected.
Comfort drawn from familiar ways, wisps of you.

It can't be, when all the flowers wilt.
The casseroles eaten, the cards sent and piled.
There remains the lonely heart.
Weighing the odds to stop or start?

For if this self that beats, declined.
Would it not be relief divine?
The lonely heart would reunite with its twin beyond.
Yet to stay, await, the natural light,
is a choice seeped in the bravery of each dawn.

FEBRUARY, 2011

Evening Song

Smiles, pause, helping hands
Lift the heart up
When harsh it lands

Hush, time, softening grace
Quiet the thunder
Offer embrace

Tend, grasp and restore
Carry the burdens
Open the door

Breathe, soothe, answer the plea
And within do pray
For a kinder me

June, 2016

Mid-Morning Tea

Life abounds
Whitecaps prance
Rain spatters
Sunrays hide
Clouds hover
Tides drift
Birds visit
Violetbells shimmer
Bees whisper
Tommy giggles
Tandem sails
Breezy chill
Smokestacks puff
Barges crawl
Flies zigzag
Mind relaxed
Soul smiles

JUNE, 2016

The Bridge

Dreams come quickly when we awaken
Cupping brisk desire and elevating hope
To splash against the cerebral canvas
Departing from routine, blurred pace and rigid demands
Only then can we fully wake up.

No screens, scrolling, tapping content
Nor hour to hour confines
Ecstasy is welcoming anonymity
The story is the breath of each unscheduled moment
Crisp, sparkling fields to dig out words, creations
Vocabulary excavations shovels of never before concepts,
piled and waiting to be ravished

Treasures unearthed with each scribble
Nibbled lovingly then hungry for the next morsel
Now awake, I fear mundane slumber
Resist the reunion with chaotic, static threads unraveling time

Acute perception tunes out verbose waste
Defiantly I must refuse sleep. But how?
Is awakening reliant on latitude and optical inspiration?
Or can the field be tended whenever, wherever,
energetically with radiant diligence?

Memory will bridge the contrasting realities
From rigorous purposeful expectations to harvesting, welcoming seeds.

This intentional duality can be possible, explored.
Sleep no more, the bright pioneering brain.
Rest when called upon to rejuvenate.
Do not neglect or abandon to fatigued martyrdom.
Yet rather be alert, adeptly cross from the "have to's"
Know tirelessly, joyfully, the dream.

The challenge is not return heartsick, but hopeful.
The bridge is constructed.

Wearing certainty as my crucifix, praying, faith making, trust in sacrifice.
Now cross over and be reunited with this adoring self peace.

JUNE, 2016

Bodaica

Chilling to pause long enough
descend to the basement of instinct.
Webs of memory, gossamer dread
force the reunion of avoidance versus truth.

Hidden, shrouded self behind smiles and piles,
mounds of doing to be bent, kicked and netted.
Score one for her.

Manifest the treasure chest, hoist the lid,
splintered not destroyed, damn the clultter of all words unsaid.
Every knowing packed away, diminished, fleeting self,
amid the fright of being right,
still a pulse to be touched, revived and heard.
Score two for her.

Tumbling to the scarred sanctuary, emotional tattoos,
honored not shamed, beauty is in the eyes of the essential woman.
Carrying herself to safety, transformed.
Bodaica rescue, collects her heart and starts, breathing out and in.
To be the knowing one, conquer, Win.

January, 2017

The End of This Beginning

ABOUT THE GRATITUDE

I am a very fortunate soul to deeply, completely and with mounds of ongoing appreciation acknowledge the support orbiting my life. Each and everyone, and many others not mentioned, all contributors to being spectacularly, eternally "love able."

Kelly, my best friend, sister and cherished illustrator of this work: You show me how art is a lifeline to fulfillment. I am grateful for your reliable source of loving encouragement, pee pants worthy humor and direct compassionate wake up calls reminding me to fill my creative bucket with my words because they are worth owning and sharing.

Meaghen, my Dr. Watson*: Your gentle nudges, wise reflections, tireless technical prowess and unflinching faith in my talents makes for a friendship for the ages, you by my side investigating the mystery of creative expression.

Anita L., Ann G., Carol K., Cindy, Cynthia, Jackie, Janet, Janice, Jean, Jennifer M., Karen, Kelly L., Lisa, Lynda, Patti C., Penny V., Suzanne, all my Brigids**: I share a unique history overflowing with gorgeous gifts of your friendship, urging and applauding my talents, challenging my procrastination, providing feedback and lovingly holding me accountable and true.

Tommy, my BooBoo: From conception to today, the most significant inspiration, vibrant joy, revelatory guide to helping me stretch and become the best version of me. Love is not a big enough word and there is never enough time.

Mark, my hubby: Your enduring calm and prolific encouragement are anchors when I get lost in the nightmarish seas of self-doubt. You wake me up and tell me to keep writing, going and dreaming. You are my heart's safe space.

My Angels, Mum and Dad: All I am able to be is due to your loving me.

*Watson: Dr. Watson, Sherlock Holmes companion, partner and friend.

**Brigid: Celtic goddess Brigid, known as a goddess of healers, poets, smiths, childbirth and inspiration. Her name means "exalted one."

ABOUT THE AUTHOR

Born in Montreal, Canada and moving to Southern California in elementary school, Julie (Juls) started spinning tales in 4th grade. She was given one composition booklet and immediately asked the teacher for two more, as there was a fantasy trilogy brewing the minute "use your imagination" prompt was assigned. At 16, her father's work transported her family to the Central African Republic, later opening doors to travel throughout Europe during her early 20s, packing journals before toothpaste.

Combining wordsmith fascination with perennial inner exploration, Julie was at home as a student, completing her thesis for a Master of Arts in Counseling Psychology and a dissertation for a Doctorate in Psychology. Pen to paper was the vehicle to introspection and as a licensed psychotherapist for over 30 years, Dr. Juls incorporates writing as a soothing agent for emotional healing and overall wellness.

Welcoming motherhood at age 41, Julie developed a deep appreciation for the challenges women face to integrate self-care while tending to the needs of children, work, family and relationships. With humor, insight and a steadfast dedication to healing, Julie offers workshops inviting women to become **Pirate Sisters** and mend buried hurts and discover lost treasures. Over the years her creative energy has expanded to her website blog and monthly **Seven Seas Messages** (www.drjuls.com).

When Julie is not meeting with clients, sitting on a seaside rock with her journal, conducting workshops or catching up on emails, she revels in precious time spent with her family, bubbly giggles with gal pals, watching British mysteries with her husband and savoring every moment with her son who soars from the nest and lands back for home cooked meals and lively conversations about healing the world's wounds.

Pirate Sisters

Purposefully **I**nitiate **R**isks **A**chieving **T**reasured **E**ssence

Come aboard and become a PIRATE Sister — enhance the beauty, fulfillment and value in your precious life.

Poetry is my treasure. In a whispered inner voice, a thought glimmers and I dig, revealing words I dust off and place on a page. As a therapist I help others discover their treasures by navigating the dark foreboding seas of ancient shame and guilt, steadying emotions in storms of self-doubt and strategize how to move forward when stuck in shallow shores anchored to regrets and fear.

When we bury our treasured self, we lose our essence. The courageous Pirate Sister is ready to bravely set intentions as sails to explore the wide expanse of possibilities and discover treasures within that have been buried and lost.

Subscribe now at www.drjuls.com

Pirate Sisters repair tattered sails, replenish supplies of hope and confidence and share in uplifting, heartbreaking, courageous, sobering and wondrous tales of surviving emotional storms and charting new directions to fulfillment.

You are a Pirate Sister. Your treasure is ready to be found.

www.ingramcontent.com/pod-product-compliance
Lightning Source LLC
Chambersburg PA
CBHW061956070426
42450CB00011BA/3121